Informed Consent

Deborah Zoe Laufer

A SAMUEL FRENCH ACTING EDITION

SAMUEL FRENCH

FOUNDED 1830

SAMUELFRENCH.COM
SAMUELFRENCH-LONDON.CO.UK

FOR PRODUCTION ENQUIRIES

UNITED STATES AND CANADA
Info@SamuelFrench.com
1-866-598-8449

UNITED KINGDOM AND EUROPE
Plays@SamuelFrench-London.co.uk
020-7255-4302

Each title is subject to availability from Samuel French, depending upon country of performance. Please be aware that *INFORMED CONSENT* may not be licensed by Samuel French in your territory. Professional and amateur producers should contact the nearest Samuel French office or licensing partner to verify availability.

MUSIC USE NOTE

Licensees are solely responsible for obtaining formal written permission from copyright owners to use copyrighted music in the performance of this play and are strongly cautioned to do so. If no such permission is obtained by the licensee, then the licensee must use only original music that the licensee owns and controls. Licensees are solely responsible and liable for all music clearances and shall indemnify the copyright owners of the play(s) and their licensing agent, Samuel French, against any costs, expenses, losses and liabilities arising from the use of music by licensees. Please contact the appropriate music licensing authority in your territory for the rights to any incidental music.

IMPORTANT BILLING AND CREDIT REQUIREMENTS

If you have obtained performance rights to this title, please refer to your licensing agreement for important billing and credit requirements.

INFORMED CONSENT was first produced in New York by Primary Stages (Casey Childs, Founder and Executive Producer; Andrew Leynse, Artistic Director; Elliot Fox, Managing Director) and Ensemble Studio Theatre (William Carden, Artistic Director; Paul Slee, Executive Director) at The Duke on 42nd Street on August 4, 2015. The performance was directed by Liesl Tommy, with sets by Wilson Chin, costumes by Jacob A. Climer, lights by Matthew Richards, sound and original music by Broken Chord, projections by Jeanette OI-Suk Yew, and props by Christine Goldman. The Production Stage Manager was Robbie Kyle Peters. The cast was as follows:

ONE	Tina Benko
TWO	Jesse J. Perez
THREE	Delanna Studi
FOUR	Pun Bandhu
FIVE	Myra Lucretia Taylor

INFORMED CONSENT received its world premiere on March 18, 2014 in a co-production between Geva Theatre Center in Rochester, New York (Mark Cuddy, Artistic Director; Tom Parrish, Executive Director) and the Cleveland Playhouse in Cleveland, Ohio (Laura Kepley, Artistic Director; Kevin Moore, Managing Director), in association with Ensemble Studio Theatre/Alfred P. Sloan Foundation Science and Technology Project. The performance was directed by Sean Daniels, with sets by Michael Raiford, costumes by Amanda Doherty, lights by Brian Lilienthal, sound by Matthew Callahan, and dramaturgy by Jenn Werner. The Production Stage Manager was Frank Cavallo and the Assistant Stage Managers were Jenny Daniels and Jenn Lyons. The Production Assistant was Stephie Kesselring. The cast was as follows:

ONE	Jessica Wortham
TWO	Fajer Al-Kaisi
THREE	Larissa FastHorse
FOUR	Gilbert Cruz
FIVE	Tina Fabrique

INFORMED CONSENT was developed with the support of PlayPenn, Paul Meshejian, Artistic Director

CHARACTERS

ONE:

JILLIAN – Genetic anthropologist. The smartest person in the room. Desperate to make the most of the time she has left to save her daughter. Full of life and hunger.

TWO:

GRAHAM – Jillian's husband, children's book author. Loving and patient. A romantic. An optimist.

THREE:

NATALIE – Jillian and Graham's four-year-old daughter
ARELLA – Spokesperson for the tribe, in her 30s.

FOUR:

KEN – A social anthropologist, in his 70s.

LAWYER
LITTLE GIRL AT THE BOOK NOOK

JOAN – A Preschool Mom

FIVE:

DEAN HAGAN,

JILLIAN'S MOTHER
SHEILA – A Preschool Mom

SETTING

Present Day.

AUTHOR'S NOTES

When there is a slash in the middle of a line / the next actor begins to speak.

There could be projections on a screen. There don't have to be.

Characters could shift with a single piece of costume. Or actors can simply morph. It should all be as fluid as possible.

The chants and rituals during the blood collection should be designed by the creative team for each production. It should be clean and simple. It must be original because performing the actual Native chant on stage is not respectful.

CASTING NOTE

The cast should be as racially diverse as possible. All best efforts should be made to cast an Indigenous actress in the role of Arella. If that is unfeasible, the role must be cast with an actress of color. If there are questions please contact Samuel French to discuss.

SPECIAL THANKS

I'm so grateful to so many people and organizations who helped me develop this piece. I can only name a fraction of them, or there wouldn't be room for the play. Ensemble Studio Theatre and the Alfred P. Sloan Foundation, Primary Stages, Geva Theatre Center, Cleveland Playhouse, PlayPenn, The Eugene O'Neill Baltic Playwrights Conference, Billy Carden, Andrew Leynse, Michelle Bossy, Linsay Firman, Graeme Gillis, Tessa LaNeve, Derek Zasky, Jenni Werner, Amy Cordileone, Liesl Tommy, Kyle Brown, Sean Daniels, my brilliant writers' groups, and, most of all, David, Alex and Charlie.

For Dr. Ben Stanger

(JILLIAN *is composing a letter to her daughter,* NATALIE. *It is difficult to find the words.*)

JILLIAN. Dear Natalie. Once upon a time…

> *(She pauses. The cast, as her pulse, as her DNA, as her story, whispers behind her.)*

TWO. TA

FOUR. GC

FIVE. CG

THREE. AT

FIVE. GC

> *(And on and on, repeated in this order, at a whisper.)*

JILLIAN. …there was a mother. Who had a monster sleeping inside her.

> *(The cast stops the genome. This is not right at all.)*

FIVE. No, no, no.

JILLIAN. Ugh. That's awful.

FOUR. Yeah.

TWO. It's just not *you.* That's not how you tell it.

JILLIAN. OK.

TWO. It's more how I would tell it, actually.

FIVE. Try again.

JILLIAN. OK.

> *(breath)*

Once upon a time

> *(The pulse, once again, beneath her words at a whisper:)*

TWO. TA

FOUR. GC

FIVE. CG

THREE. AT

FIVE. GC

JILLIAN. …there was a little girl, whose mother loved her so much…

TWO. Good.

JILLIAN. …that she would do anything to save her.

THREE. No matter who got hurt.

TWO. Hey.

FOUR. Come on.

FIVE. That's definitely not how she'd tell it.

THREE. That's how I'd tell it.

FIVE. I know. But tonight…

THREE. Yeah?

FIVE. Tonight might be the last time she can tell it.

> *(beat)*

Go back.

TWO. Start with the couple.

THREE. Start with the tribe.

FOUR. Start with the university.

FIVE. Start with the scientist.

ALL. Once upon a time…

FIVE. *(helping her)* Once upon a time at a large university in Arizona, there was a scientist.

JILLIAN. *(immediately needing control of the story)* Well, a genetic anthropologist. Actually.

FIVE. Fine. A genetic anthropolo/gist.

JILLIAN. Who was the smartest person in the room.

FIVE. *(sardonically amused)* OK.

TWO. She had a husband

THREE. And a daughter

FOUR. And a pendant

FIVE. Her mother died much too young.

JILLIAN. She was afraid of horses. Seriously.

FOUR. This genetic anthropologist loved to say...

JILLIAN. We're family!

THREE. She looo/oved...

FOUR. She loved to say that.

FIVE. She made a *lot* of speeches.

JILLIAN. We're all cousins! It's genetic. It's a *fact*!

THREE. She believed in *facts*.

JILLIAN. Now that we can trace our genome, we're finally able to read the greatest story every told – the history of our species, written in our cells. And what is it telling us? That we're all cousins! There is a single mutation in the genes of every one of us that we can trace back to one woman in Africa, only a hundred fifty thousand years ago.
We call her

ALL. Mitochondrial Eve.

JILLIAN. She was our great great /great great great...

THREE. And on and on and on...

JILLIAN. ...great great grandmother. Yours and mine.
Everyone in this room, everyone on this planet – we all share that one single mutation. From that one woman. In Africa. So...

ALL. We're all cousins!

JILLIAN. And...
We're all Africans!

(beat)

FIVE. We're all Africans.

JILLIAN. All humans are 99.9 percent the same genetically. One base pair out of three thousand between you and the guy next to you. We have so much more in common than we have differences. Really.

THREE. Really.

JILLIAN. We're so alike.

TWO. So alike.

JILLIAN. Only *.1 percent* different.

FIVE. So alike.

JILLIAN. Is that difference race? Is that .1 percent?

FIVE. skin color

JILLIAN. and

THREE. shape of eyes

JILLIAN. and

TWO. hair texture

JILLIAN. whatever you think of as "race"?

> *(All the actors make " " fingers.)*

FOUR. Nope.

JILLIAN. No! Race isn't biological. There are no genes that indicate race.

FIVE. She loved to say…

JILLIAN. "Race" *(All the actors make " " fingers.)* is a fiction. It's a myth.
All of the things we see as "race" *(All actors " ".)* are about migratory patterns!

THREE. Migratory patterns?

JILLIAN. About where our tribes went when they migrated from Africa.
Then, what is that thing, that .1 percent that makes you different from anyone else. That makes you…you?

FOUR. That makes you…

JILLIAN. Such a tiny difference.

TWO. You.

JILLIAN. But that tiny difference…

FOUR. That makes /you…

FIVE. Makes /you…

THREE. Makes you…

TWO. You.

JILLIAN. Makes all the difference.

THREE. She had a clicker, and she wasn't afraid to use it.

> *(She clicks her clicker and* TWO *makes the noise.)*

TWO. Click.

> *(A genome sequence appears on the screen.)*

JILLIAN. This is me.

TWO. A

FIVE. T

FOUR. C

THREE. G

> *(While* **JILLIAN** *speaks, the other actors softly read the sequence.)*

TWO. TA

FOUR. GC

FIVE. CG

THREE. AT

FIVE. GC

> *(And on and on, repeated in this order, at a whisper.)*

JILLIAN. That's my story, my genome.
It's also the echo of everyone who's come before me –
written in my DNA – three billion bases all made up of
adenine, thymine, cytosine and guanine. Or just ATCG
among friends.

> *(The cast stops.)*

And this... *(She clicks.)*

TWO. Click.

JILLIAN. is my mother.

> *(Another genetic sequence comes up – the cast reads it, a whisper.)*

TWO. TA

FOUR. GC

FIVE. CG

THREE. AT

FIVE. GC

JILLIAN. This...

(JILLIAN *shows her necklace. Maybe it also appears on the screen.*)

JILLIAN. This was her pendant that she always wore. That I always wear now. When she gave it to me, she thought I was her sister, Jenny. Her hands shook so much she couldn't unfasten the clasp.

FIVE. (*as* **JILLIAN'S MOTHER,** *struggling with the clasp*) You should have this, Jenny.

JILLIAN. I'm Jillian, Mama.

FIVE. This should go to you.

JILLIAN. She was only thirty-four years old.

FOUR. Thirty-four years old.

JILLIAN. As I am, today. And I was only seven.
   Later, I found one dark strand of hair caught in that clasp. Which I saved.

TWO. She saves everything.

JILLIAN. On that strand of hair was one tiny root particle. And with that tiny bit of root, over twenty years later, I traced my mother's genome. Unlocked her mysteries. Finally got to know her.

ALL. TA GC CG AT GC

JILLIAN. Stop. There. There it is. There's the glitch.
   And here it is in my genome.

TWO. Click

ALL. TA GC CG AT GC

JILLIAN. Same glitch. Mutation in the amyloid precursor protein. Chromosome 21. Right there. Familial. Inherited. Early onset. Alzheimer's.

   (*Beat. Light shift.*)

TWO. Once upon a time, at the floor of the Grand Canyon, there was a tribe of Native

ARELLA. Native.

TWO. Americans.

ARELLA. Americans. That's your word. Not ours.

FIVE. There was a tribe who lived at the floor of the Grand Canyon.

ARELLA. We sprang forth from the Grand Canyon.

FIVE. And, in that same large university in the state of Arizona there was a social anthropologist...

> *(FOUR hurriedly steps forward, claiming the role.)*

...in his seventies.

FOUR. In his *seventies?*

> *(He adjusts his posture to reflect his age.)*

FIVE. He called the genetic anthropologist into his office.

> *(A slide of KEN's office, appears on one side of the screen. His genome is on the other side.)*

FOUR. *(becoming KEN)* I called Doctor Elliott into my office. Hard-working, passionate young woman, if a little...

THREE. Fanatical?

KEN. Overzealous. She reminds me of my daughter at that age. When my contact from the Public Health School moved to Singapore, I immediately thought of Dr. Elliott as a replacement. Seemed like the perfect opportunity for a young person with fire in her belly, you know?

> *(to JILLIAN, delighted to talk about his favorite subject)*

The beauty of the place, Jillian.

JILLIAN. *(overwhelmed, thrilled)* Oh my God.

KEN. And the people.

JILLIAN. Ken!

KEN. They're a remarkable people.

> *(JILLIAN impulsively hugs him in her excitement. He's unprepared for this, but pleased.)*

JILLIAN. Thank you!! Thank you so much! I'm so thrilled you came to me!

JILLIAN. *(to the audience)* I don't even have tenure yet, and he's handing over this massive opportunity?! I hope he realizes that diabetes isn't my field of study.

KEN. I realize that diabetes isn't your field of study. You're working on...

JILLIAN. Right. Gene flow based on migratory patterns.

KEN. Ah! All these new fields!

JILLIAN. Some day I'd actually like to be focusing on Alzheimers full-time, but, you know, at this stage, every opportunity is wonderful.

KEN. Well, like I always tell my daughter – you just keep putting one foot in front of the other, slow and sure, and there's no limit to how far you can go.

JILLIAN. Until you reach the ocean!

> *(He looks at her blankly.)*

I won't let you down, Ken. You'll see.

KEN. *(his book)* I want you to have this.

JILLIAN. Oh. Thanks!

KEN. *(to the audience)* I gave her my book. Inscribed, of course.

> *(to* JILLIAN*)*

As you can see, I've inscribed it.

JILLIAN. Wow! Thank you!

KEN. This will give you a sense of the history of the tribe, their form of self-government, their creation story.

ARELLA. We sprang forth from the Grand /Canyon.

JILLIAN. That's great, thanks! So... I guess we should make an amendment to the IRB?

> *(to the audience)*

Institutional Review Board

> *(to* KEN*)*

To reflect the change in personnel?

ARELLA. We were the first people on Earth. My people.

KEN. Of course it charts their relationship with and therefore distrust of the white man.

JILLIAN. Of course.

KEN. *(reading from the back flap of his book)* We raped them of their land, their way of life.

JILLIAN. It's awful, Ken. I can't wait to read it.

KEN. Good!

JILLIAN. I was looking at the work that the NIH did with the Pima – there are some striking similarities. The tribe's degree of isolation, their rate of diabetes. Boy, if we find the same candidate gene –

KEN. Yes?

JILLIAN. We could really help them, you know? Get them the right treatment. Fast.

KEN. You're already on the case!

JILLIAN. I'm on it!

So, when could I get a team down to start collecting samples? How would I get them down there?

KEN. You've never been?

JILLIAN. No.

(We see images of the Grand Canyon on the screen.)

KEN. You live on the lip of the Grand Canyon, one of the great natural wonders of the world, and you've never / gone?

JILLIAN. I've been meaning to, but you know…life…

KEN. You've got to lift your eyes up from that microscope, young lady!

JILLIAN. You're so right! I will!

KEN. Good. So, there are three ways to get down there. You can climb down by foot, which is around an eight-mile hike.

JILLIAN. Wow.

KEN. Just magnificent. You can ride in by horseback.

JILLIAN. Hmmm…

KEN. Or there are regular helicopter runs.

JILLIAN. OK! Helicopter is sounding awesome.

> *(to the audience)*

I had this incident when I was a kid – horseback riding. We were in this indoor rink, and it was /winter and icy...

> (**FIVE** *coughs.*)

FIVE. Not really relevant...

KEN. There are regular helicopter runs bringing down supplies...

JILLIAN. If I can get all the paperwork done – consent forms, can we get down there next week?

> *(pulling out her iPhone)*

I have Wednesday afternoons open. So...do you know when the next helicopter run is? Do they have a regular /schedule or...

KEN. Whoa. This is going to take some time, Jillian. We need to handle this very delicately.

JILLIAN. OK...

KEN. They've never allowed blood to be taken for any kind of research.

ARELLA. Our blood is sacred.

JILLIAN. Maybe if I could go down there, talk to them...

KEN. Jillian, I've spent forty years with this tribe. They're my family.

JILLIAN. *(to the audience)* Well, we're all family, really.

KEN. Their creation story tells of how they sprang forth from the Grand Canyon. They're its guardians. They don't easily let white people into their community.

JILLIAN. *(to the audience)* There's no such thing as "white" people, really. *(The whole cast does " ".)*

ARELLA. When I was little, before I'd met Ken, I'd hear about, "the white man did this and the white man did that." I thought there was one white man and he did all these terrible things. Like, if they had just locked up that awful white man everything would have been great.

KEN. I earned their trust. A sacred trust.

JILLIAN. And they came to you for help. Which is fantastic. That they could turn to you.

KEN. I lived there in the canyon for over a year in the 60s.

(to the audience)

Back then I was just beginning my field work. I'd recently graduated – no wife, no family, and I was heading west on /my way to…

FIVE. Again, this is really not your story.

KEN. So far nine people have consented to giving samples.

JILLIAN. *(to the audience) Nine* participants? And he calls it a *study?*

KEN. There are only six hundred seventy tribe members left.

JILLIAN. *(to the audience)* Well, he's a social anthropologist That's just barely science, really.

KEN. This will take patience, Jillian. For most of the tribe the thought of giving their blood is…unthinkable. It could take up to a year or two for you to gain their trust, help them /warm to the idea.

JILLIAN. A *year* or two???

FIVE. *(becoming* JILLIAN'S MOTHER*)*

(struggling to unhook her pendant)

You should have this, Jenny.

JILLIAN. I'm Jillian, Mama. Not Jenny. Aunt Jenny died.

JILLIAN'S MOTHER. This should belong to you, Jenny. I can't… Ahh…it's stuck! I can't…

(She backs away.)

JILLIAN. Ken! They don't have a year or two. I mean, it's an epidemic – almost fifty percent of the population. Let me get down there. I'll bring some literature… /the success with the Pimas…

KEN. English is not their first language.

ARELLA. We're the only remaining tribe in the country whose tribal language is our first language.

JILLIAN. I'll bring a translator.

KEN. Arella Namida is working on convincing the tribal council. I've known her since she was a little girl. She's becoming a real force there.

JILLIAN. Could I just meet with her then? Arella...

KEN. I taught her how to drive.

ARELLA. There are no cars in my village. He insisted I come to the plateau. That I learn to drive.

KEN. She's like a daughter to me.

JILLIAN. Wow. /That's...

ARELLA. Only five tribe members have ever graduated from college. He insisted I go.

KEN. Like my own daughter.

JILLIAN. She sounds remarkable. How would I contact her? Arella...

KEN. She'll convince them. I feel almost certain.

(*Beat, as* **JILLIAN** *works to control her hunger.*)

JILLIAN. OK. In the meantime, I'll get those documents to the IRB – stress the /urgency that we begin...

KEN. You know Dr. Elliott, this is strictly a diabetes study.

JILLIAN. (*to the audience*) I don't think he said that.

KEN. I did. I remember...

JILLIAN. Not "strictly" (*The cast does " ".*)

KEN. Fine. You know Dr. Elliott, this is a diabetes study.

JILLIAN. Yes. I'm so glad you came to me Ken. No one here has worked more with human subjects. Oh – should we also put together a nutritional program? Who is that nutritionist...she was working in Carl's lab.

KEN. Yeah...

JILLIAN. Do we have funding for that? What do they eat down there?

KEN. Their diet is not what it was. You'll see in the book /how they...

JILLIAN. Right. Good.

KEN. Hunter-gatherers. Farmers.

ARELLA. There was a time my sister could climb the whole canyon to the rim in three hours. /Now…

KEN. Now, few of the tribe can climb any more.

JILLIAN. Right.

KEN. Health, weight, /amputations.

ARELLA. Amputations.

JILLIAN. I'll put a good team together. You can count on it.

> *(light shift)*

> *(To the audience:)*

Stay healthy, cousins. Stay healthy for the next twenty years. Don't get hit by a bus, resist french fries, wear a seat belt – you might live to see…*two hundred.*

And, if research continues at the incredible rate it's going, it's possible… (I really shouldn't even say this. Cone of silence, OK?) it's possible that our children's children will attain…immortality.

I know, it sounds crazy! Believe me, I know! But genomic progress is sprinting forward at super exponential speeds. It's breathtaking. The first genome sequencing in 2003 cost about three billion dollars. In a few years, you'll carry around a card with your entire sequence on it for a thousand bucks.

FIVE. *(becoming* **DEAN HAGAN***)* The Dean of the large university in Arizona was a little uncomfortable with these assertions.

> *(to* **JILLIAN***)*

I'm not really comfortable with the assertions you've been making publically. You said we're about to become immortal?

JILLIAN. Oh. No. Hah! Well, I said that our rate of progress is exponential and that, you know, that there's really no knowing what might be possible. In the future.

DEAN HAGAN. Let's just stick to science, Dr. Elliott, and let the English department imagine the unimaginable.

JILLIAN. Okey dokey.

  (to the audience)

Our Dean – a visionary.

Where was I?

  (She can't remember. It's a bit unnerving. Pause.)

THREE. *(trying to help her, a whisper)* Exponential growth…

  (This doesn't help. Pause. The cast looks to each other, worried.)

FOUR. Stay healthy cousins…

  (JILLIAN is still lost.)

TWO. God of Cancer.

JILLIAN. Oh. Right! Thanks. OK. OK, so, the way we treat disease today – it's still the Dark Ages. We throw chemicals at a problem and pray that the God of Cancer will make it go away. Seriously – we're basically poisoning people to see if we can kill off the disease before we kill off the person.

But once we can read your genome, we're going to be able to find out exactly what's malfunctioning in *your* body. And the pharmacist will whip up a drug specifically for you. We could end disease. We could re-grow aging cell tissue. It's all within our grasp.

This is why it's so important that we all take part. That we all give our blood. I mean, my genome is up on the internet for anyone to look at. Because really, it's *our* DNA. *Our* history. *Our* stories.

We're all in this together, cousins. To save us all. The human family.

  (light shift)

TWO. *(becoming* **GRAHAM***)*

  (He is telling the story to **NATALIE**, *his daughter.)*

Once upon a time a man and a woman fell in love. The man was the color of the earth's deep clay, and the woman had skin like soft ripe peaches. And they came together with so much love, sooo much love, that...

THREE. *(as* **NATALIE***)* They had a little girl!

GRAHAM. They had a little girl. And that little girl was the smartest, funniest, kindest...

NATALIE. Best singing!

GRAHAM. best singing, most generous little girl who ever lived. She was also beautiful, which isn't as important as those other things, but may as well be mentioned.

(*light shift*)

FOUR. The genetic anthropologist told her /husband

FIVE. And told him and told him and /told him

FOUR. about the restricted gene pool.

(**GRAHAM** *is searching through stacks of paper, a bit frantically, for* **NATALIE***'s poster. He has been at it for a while and is retracing.* **JILLIAN** *is following him around, out of her head excited.*)

JILLIAN. A restricted gene pool like this – it's a gold mine!

GRAHAM. Yeah?

God, where could I have put it??

JILLIAN. Looking at that DNA unpolluted – it makes what's there so /much clearer.

THREE. Unpolluted?

GRAHAM. Unpolluted... That /sounds...

JILLIAN. No no no, it's like, you're scanning the night sky, looking for a specific star?

GRAHAM. Uh, huh.

JILLIAN. If there's light pollution, like in a city, it's much harder to find it.

GRAHAM. K.

JILLIAN. Clearing away all the other light makes your star shine brighter. That's what their blood is – it's clear of all the other distractions.

GRAHAM. Aww. Who says you're not a poet, babe.

(He comes over and kisses her, and then goes back to his hunt. She is now exhilarated!)

JILLIAN. This is pretty much the oldest blood on the continent!

THREE. We were the first people.

GRAHAM. You're sure you haven't seen Natalie's picture?

THREE. Our blood is sacred.

JILLIAN. This is how it happens hon – huge breakthroughs in science – when large related families like this allow research. That's how we identified the gene for Huntingtons.

GRAHAM. Yeah?

JILLIAN. This group of families in Venezuela gave their blood. The Mormons In Salt Lake City gave us the key to colon cancer.

GRAHAM. Huh.

JILLIAN. And this tribe is much more isolated. So – who knows what we'll discover here. This could majorly impact genomic research. And we could save the tribe from extinction. Which is where they're headed. Fast.

GRAHAM. Amazing.

(his search)

How is this possible? I left it right here.

JILLIAN. Oh my God. Maybe I could get a *Cell* article, Graham.

GRAHAM. Hmm.

JILLIAN. Maybe even *Nature*. And if that happens… Oh my God.

GRAHAM. What?

JILLIAN. I could finally get funding for my own lab. Focus on Alzheimer's full time.

GRAHAM. Whoa…

JILLIAN. With all my focus, and the right funding, – which an article in *Nature* would generate – oh my God. I could cure it.

GRAHAM. Whoa… Honey. Slow down. You just went from doing this study on…

THREE & FOUR. Diabetes

GRAHAM. On diabetes, to getting your own lab, to curing Alzheimers… It's kind of…a big leap, right? I mean…

JILLIAN. You only get one opportunity like this in a lifetime, hon – it could change my whole career. My whole life. Change Natalie's life.

> (emotional)

I'm going to save her, Graham. I am.

GRAHAM. (a little worried that she's spiraled out of control) OK, hon.

JILLIAN. (back to her impassioned planning) I'll need to test for a lot of things – schizophrenia, alcoholism, I'll take handprints.

GRAHAM. Handprints?

JILLIAN. That's how we find patterns for inbreeding.

THREE & FOUR. Inbreeding?

FOUR. This is strictly a diabetes study.

JILLIAN & FIVE. You didn't say "strictly"

GRAHAM. Where is that drawing?!

JILLIAN. You checked her room?

GRAHAM. It's not there.

JILLIAN. Huh.

GRAHAM. I left it right here. Last night.

JILLIAN. Weird.

> (beat)

Did I tell you, they have the third highest rate of Type 2 diabetes *in the world*?

GRAHAM. Maybe you should sound less gleeful about it.

JILLIAN. Graham, I could really help them.

GRAHAM. Honey. Are you sure you haven't seen it?

JILLIAN. What does it look like?

GRAHAM. *(a little incredulous)* Her *poster*. Of *us*. The one she's been working on all week.

JILLIAN. I don't think so.

GRAHAM. Shit. She's going to fail preschool and it's all my fault. Could you have moved it? Or thrown it out?

JILLIAN. Me? Throw something /out?

FIVE. *(to the audience)* She saves everything.

GRAHAM. Could you see if it's in with your papers?

JILLIAN. Why would it be in with /my papers?

GRAHAM. Because it's not anywhere else?! Help me out here!

JILLIAN. OK! OK!

> *(She looks through her briefcase and finds it.)*

Oh my God.

GRAHAM. Jillian! Jesus! I've been looking for an hour!

JILLIAN. Look at this.

GRAHAM. What?

> (JILLIAN *turns the painting around. We see it on the screen. It shows a four-year-old's drawing of her family – the daddy and girl are brown, holding hands. The mommy is white, and off by herself.)*

JILLIAN. This is how she sees us.

GRAHAM. I know – I'm *significantly* smaller than you.

JILLIAN. Graham. I'm...separate.

GRAHAM. Just a bit.

JILLIAN. You're both brown and holding hands, and I'm white. And separate. She thinks I'm different. A different...race.

GRAHAM. She doesn't know about race hon. She just draws what she sees. I was here with her while she was coloring it, and you /were at work.

JILLIAN. It looks like... "One of these things is not like the other." Like I got sorted out.

GRAHAM. No.

JILLIAN. I'm away too much. I work too much.

GRAHAM. She's just going through a Daddy's girl phase. Every little girl goes through that.

JILLIAN. I didn't.

GRAHAM. *(giving her a hug)* Well, you're a freak.

FIVE. Wait. Back it up a little. Give us some context.

JILLIAN. *(to the audience)* I didn't think we should have a child. I told him that first day, the day we met.

FOUR. Do the meeting. In the bookstore. I love that part.

> (**THREE** *steps forward to grab a prop.*)

Nah, that's OK. I'll be the little girl.

THREE. *(laughs)* Sounds good.

GRAHAM. She was standing at the back of Book Nook. I was giving a reading of my book "Lily the Lemming" to the kids. Now, the book is hilarious. It's about this lemming who decides she's not going to follow the pack /and the rest of the lemmings…

FIVE. *(coughs)* Anyway…

GRAHAM. Anyway, you're just going to have to trust me – it's killer funny. I mean, all the kids are cracking up and she's just standing there in the back, watching. It was a little creepy really.

JILLIAN. I laughed.

GRAHAM. No.

JILLIAN. I did! I remember. I thought /it was funny…

GRAHAM. OK, hon.

JILLIAN. *(to the audience)* What made me stop to listen? I don't know. Between us – I'd just gone in to use the bathroom.

> (**FOUR**, *now a little girl with a cold, hands* **GRAHAM** *a book to sign.*)

FOUR. Emiwy.

GRAHAM. Very nice to meet you, Emily.

> (*He signs the book.*)

FOUR. *(She sneezes on and then gives him a picture she's drawn.)* I dwew this. Wiwy.

GRAHAM. Wow! You drew Lily!

JILLIAN. He knew – what to say to them.

GRAHAM. It's amazing. Is this for me?

> *(She nods.)*

Thank you so much! I'll hang it on my fridge!

> *(**FOUR** moves away and **JILLIAN** approaches.)*

JILLIAN. *(her version of flirting)* That was pretty good. I mean, your story. For fiction. I usually hate fiction.

GRAHAM. Who says it's fiction?

JILLIAN. Hah!

GRAHAM. So…you're…here by yourself?

JILLIAN. Me? Yeah.

GRAHAM. At a children's book reading?

JILLIAN. Oh. Right. Yeah.

GRAHAM. You don't have kids?

JILLIAN. No. No. I don't. I won't…have kids.

GRAHAM. OK…

JILLIAN. Ever.

GRAHAM. OK…

FOUR. Later, at her apartment…

> *(**JILLIAN** and **GRAHAM** are making out.)*

JILLIAN. *(disentangling)* I need to tell you something.

GRAHAM. I need to tell *you* something.

JILLIAN. What?

GRAHAM. You're adorable.

> *(He tries to resume kissing her.)*

JILLIAN. No, but really. This is serious.

GRAHAM. You are *seriously* adorable.

JILLIAN. Graham.

GRAHAM. Jillian.

JILLIAN. I have to tell you this. It's important.

GRAHAM. You're a dude, aren't you.

JILLIAN. No.

GRAHAM. Excellent!

> *(tries to kiss her again)*

JILLIAN. Graham. You should know this if we're gonna move forward.

GRAHAM. It can't wait for the second date?

JILLIAN. You may not want a second date.

GRAHAM. But I've already cleared my calendar.

JILLIAN. There's a fifty percent chance I'll get early-onset Alzheimers.

GRAHAM. *(laughing)* OK...

JILLIAN. *(to the audience)* This was before you could get your genome traced. Before I found out that there's one hundred percent chance.

FIVE. *Nearly /*one hundred percent.

JILLIAN. One hundred percent.

GRAHAM. Wow. Well. That's not what I was expecting.

> *(beat)*

No, seriously? I mean, you seem fine to me.

JILLIAN. My mom died of it at thirty-six. So...

GRAHAM. Oh, shit. I'm sorry.

JILLIAN. So the thing is...marrying me might mean you would have to /take care of me

GRAHAM. Whoa – *marrying* you!?

JILLIAN. for the next maybe thirty or forty years. And, I might not even know who you are.

GRAHAM. Jill, you barely know who I am now.

JILLIAN. And we couldn't have children. Our offspring would have a twenty-five percent chance of getting the disease.

GRAHAM. This is...totally...the weirdest first date ever.

Do you ever get a second date?

JILLIAN. Not often.

    (beat)

GRAHAM. OK. So good. So I know. You want to catch a movie tomorrow night?

JILLIAN. I have a lab meeting tomorrow night.

GRAHAM. *(to the audience)* I had never met anyone like her. Anyone. She says whatever's on her mind. Here are the facts, sir. No filter. Right up front. I love that… /She's…

JILLIAN. But I'm free Friday.

GRAHAM. Friday it is.

    (He goes back to kiss her. She turns to the audience.)

JILLIAN. What if we had met just a few years later when we learned the true percentages?

FOUR. One hundred percent

FIVE. Nearly…

JILLIAN. Would he have been as sure then?

GRAHAM. Yes! Life is short. There are no guarantees for any of us. I want to be with you.

FOUR. Nearly one hundred percent chance she'll get the disease.

JILLIAN. He's the optimist.

GRAHAM. I love you Jillian.

JILLIAN. The romantic.

    I'm not genetically programmed for optimism and romance.

GRAHAM. I love you. I want to marry you.

JILLIAN. So, we were married!

GRAHAM. I want a baby.

JILLIAN. No.

GRAHAM. I want to have your baby.

JILLIAN. No! No, no, no. No!

    Again, this was before *I* could be tested, or have *her* tested in-utero. So much has changed in four years. Life is so much more complicated now. Or so much simpler.

GRAHAM. *(He wraps his arms around her from behind.)* Look, the earth could be hit by an asteroid tomorrow.

JILLIAN. But what's if it's not? Then we have to deal with the day after tomorrow.

GRAHAM. I don't want to know the future.

JILLIAN. I want to know everything. Everything there is to know. More.

GRAHAM. I just want to really live, Jillian. Completely. With you. I want us to have a baby. Together. Everything we are, the good and the bad. In one small person.

JILLIAN. Twenty-five percent.

GRAHAM. Yes! We have a seventy-five percent chance that everything will go right!

JILLIAN. *(to the audience)* What were the percentages I would meet someone like that? Graham. My story could have been so different.

FOUR. *(romance novel style)* And she died alone, forever pessimistic, forever unromantic.

JILLIAN. What if he'd read "Lily the Leming" a week later? An hour? A minute? What if I hadn't eaten the bag of chips that made me drink that second iced tea that made me duck into the Book Nook to use the bathroom? What if I'd done my post-doc work in Cambridge, like I'd hoped to?

It wouldn't have been me, it wouldn't have been Graham. There would never have been Natalie. But it all happened. Just this way. This is my story. It's miraculous. I met the love of my life. At Book Nook.

GRAHAM. The love of my life.

JILLIAN. And it was so obvious –

GRAHAM. I want to have your baby.

JILLIAN. – the tragedy of someone like Graham not having a child was so much greater than that twenty-five percent. It was… Five hundred percent! So I took the leap. We did. Together.

FOUR. That was awesome! Thanks. OK…carry on.

(There's a beat as they try to get back on track.)

THREE. Natalie's picture.

JILLIAN. Right!

I'm away too much. I work too much.

GRAHAM. She's just going through a Daddy's girl phase.

JILLIAN. I need to bond with her more. You're much more bonded. I want to be more bonded.

GRAHAM. OK, hon.

JILLIAN. I'm going to do something with her this weekend! Maybe the zoo. Or the planetarium!

GRAHAM. She has birthday parties.

JILLIAN. Crap. Why do we have to have a popular kid?

GRAHAM. Sorry.

JILLIAN. That's totally your gene pool.

GRAHAM. Remind me to pick up presents tomorrow.

JILLIAN. Give them copies of your books! Give them Lily!

GRAHAM. Nah – I'll find something at Toy Barn.

JILLIAN. Hey, maybe I'll take her to the parties. Some mommy time. What was that class you did with her?

GRAHAM. Mommy and Me. Won't you be working this weekend?

JILLIAN. I can take a few hours off.

GRAHAM. It's a princess party.

JILLIAN. Ugh.

GRAHAM. At Party Palace.

JILLIAN. Look, if you can do it, I can do it.

GRAHAM. These moms Jill…

JILLIAN. What?

GRAHAM. It's just a very different culture. You might need inoculations first.

JILLIAN. What do you mean?

GRAHAM. They are *obsessed* with their kids.

JILLIAN. So? I'm obsessed with my kid. You don't think I'm obsessed with my kid?

GRAHAM. It's just...

JILLIAN. I'm totally obsessed with my kid. It's Natalie, right?

GRAHAM. Hah.

JILLIAN. I'm obsessed. I'm just not bonded.

GRAHAM. OK.

JILLIAN. I'll do it. I'll take her.

GRAHAM. Good.

> *(light shift)*

FIVE. The genetic anthropologist decided to ignore the wishes of the social anthropologist...

FOUR. This requires patience, Jillian.

FIVE. and went by herself to meet with Arella Namida. By helicopter.

> *(The sound of the helicopter.* **JILLIAN** *approaches* **ARELLA.** *)*

JILLIAN. Arella? Hi! I'm Dr. Elliott. Or... Jillian...call me. Thank you so much for meeting with me.

ARELLA. Ken didn't come with you? The message you left said /you were with...

JILLIAN. Yeah, I thought I should just come down myself this time – you know, maybe you and I could fast-track it a little. Wow. That helicopter. That was terrifying.

ARELLA. You should ride out – horseback. It's much more relaxing.

JILLIAN. Hah. Yeah. Not for me so much. I had this incident when I was a kid. I was in this indoor rink, it was winter, and this giant icicle comes down and hits my horse square on the ass and...

> *(***FIVE*** *coughs loudly.)*

Right.

So! I'm hoping that you and I can plot together a bit. You know? Figure out how to convince the council to move forward, ASAP! Or maybe *I* could just talk to them...myself?

(ARELLA doesn't respond to this. JILLIAN grabs some papers from her briefcase, gives them to ARELLA.)

JILLIAN. I brought some really persuasive literature – articles about the Pima.

(showing her)

Here – OK, as you probably know, the Pima were suffering an almost comparable rate of diabetes. I'm sure Ken told you about this.

ARELLA. No.

JILLIAN. Oh! Wow. OK. Well…they were! And…they're an isolated population that probably had a migratory pattern similar to yours.

ARELLA. Migratory pattern.

JILLIAN. Right! We'll need to find out how isolated your tribe has been. There are several studies we'll need to do to find the factors that are at play if there's a mutation in your DNA. Does that make sense?

ARELLA. I can tell you we're isolated. We've always lived /here in…

JILLIAN. Well, eight hundred years is a long time, but… always…

(ARELLA is silent.)

The thing is, there's so much you can't tell us that your blood can. Your entire history.

ARELLA. We know our history. We pass it on story by story. Generation by generation.

JILLIAN. Right. And of course your stories are meaningful and…and relevant. But, I mean, you *are* your DNA. Your genome can tell us your *whole* history.

ARELLA. Look, Doctor Elliott. We don't need you to tell us our history. We need you to find out why the tribe is dying.

(beat)

JILLIAN. Maybe if I could talk to the council…

ARELLA. Yeah, that's not a great idea.

JILLIAN. If you could tell me what their concerns are... because, there really are no risks here. We take some blood, maybe your handprints, and that's all. A needle prick is the only real harm. So, the possible good that could come from it so far outweighs the risks that...

ARELLA. We believe our blood is sacred.

JILLIAN. OK...

ARELLA. So what *you* believe to be no /risk...

JILLIAN. But, it's constantly renewing itself in your body. You give us some samples, and your body generates more.

ARELLA. We believe that if you aren't buried with your blood, your soul won't rest. It will never get to the spirit world.

JILLIAN. But that's just a myth, right? I mean, you don't actually *believe* that.

> (*beat*)

ARELLA. It's what our elders tell our children. And what our children will tell their children.

JILLIAN. ...Yes. OK. And, keeping your heritage alive is really important. Of course. But, getting to the truth is important too, right?

ARELLA. Every tribe has its own truth.

JILLIAN. Well...every tribe has its own story. But, there's really only one *truth*.

> (*beat*)

ARELLA. I'll look at the literature. Thank you for coming.

JILLIAN. No, Arella. Wait!
I want to help your tribe. And to help your tribe, I'll need to collect your blood. So, please – help me understand how to make that possible.

ARELLA. I don't think you can understand.

JILLIAN. You asked us for help. You came to us to see if there was a genetic component.

ARELLA. I asked Ken for help. I would prefer to work with him. Thank you.

JILLIAN. But he doesn't do this kind of work. That's why came to me.

Arella. You're facing an epidemic here. This may be your tribe's last, best chance. Please. Tell me how to make it OK with the council to give their blood. So we can find out what's going wrong.

    (beat)

What better choice do you have?

    (pause)

ARELLA. Look, in order to work with us, to gain the trust of the tribal council, you're going to have to understand – we have customs. We have an ancient way of life.

JILLIAN. OK, but, are you living your ancient way of life? Most of your tribe can't hunt or gather any more – you can't climb the canyon. Every year more people lose a limb, or have to leave for dialysis. Modern science, as painful as this is, might be the only way to help you regain your ancient way of life.

    (**ARELLA** *is upset, but silent.*)

I waited up there for the helicopter, and I saw the boxes and boxes of crap that's sent down here. Huge blocks of cheese and white bread. I'm sure all that processed food is not what you ate eight hundred years ago. So, tell the council – let's do the studies, look at the genetic component, and we could also offer classes in nutrition, exercise, maybe you can get some of your ancient ways /back.

ARELLA. *(furious)* Classes in nutrition. You think we want to be eating that garbage?

JILLIAN. Well, I don't think anyone /wants to be…

ARELLA. You think we wouldn't rather be hunting and farming our own food like we did for a thousand years? On our own land? Seven million acres was our territory.

Seven *million*. All of Cataract Canyon. Until you cut us down to nothing.

JILLIAN. But, I mean…there's still a lot of land to farm… it looks like.

ARELLA. You put restrictions on our water access! How could we farm? During dry times, the cattle died. The crops died.

JILLIAN. Ah. I didn't realize…

ARELLA. Yeah. By the time we got back a few thousand acres – and we had to fight for decades to get them back – we hadn't farmed for generations. We'd become dependent on tourism. What else could we do?

JILLIAN. Right.

ARELLA. You took away our livelihood, and now you mock us for eating the garbage you ship in.

JILLIAN. Arella. I'm not mocking you.

ARELLA. "You really believe that?" That's what you said. "You really believe that?" As if we're stupid. Ignorant.

JILLIAN. Wow. That's not what I meant. At all.

ARELLA. I'm so tired of you deciding, if we don't believe what you believe, we're primitive. Uneducated. We have "myths" and you have "truth."

JILLIAN. I don't think that. And I know you're educated. I mean, obviously /you're…

ARELLA. You talk about your truth. You know, there's always a new truth. The latest scientific breakthrough. The new discovery. And then a few years later, it's disproven, and there's a newer truth. Well, we've believed what we believe for a thousand years, and it's sustained us through some very bad times.

So, don't come here. To my home. And say to me "you really believe that? You really teach your children that?"

We teach our children generosity and respect. Honor the elders. Keep our traditions alive. Because this is our heritage. This is our life. Stop taking and taking and taking away our life.

JILLIAN. I'm sorry, Arella. But, I didn't take those things from you. I'm sorry that was done to you, to your people. It's unforgiveable. But – what was done is done. It's the past. We need to look to the /future.

ARELLA. To you it's the past. Look around. We're living it. Now. We're dying. Right now. It's not the past. It's tomorrow.

JILLIAN. But that's why there's no time – we need to start these studies right away.

ARELLA. If I convince them to give you our blood, you find the…gene. And then you cure it?

JILLIAN. Well, if we find evidence for the causative gene, we might be able to address risk factors.

ARELLA. And then…

JILLIAN. And then we'll know who's very likely to get diabetes and why. We'll be able to offer treatment sooner. The proper medications. We'd be able to alter diet in a way to affect that form of diabetes.

ARELLA. So…taking our blood, finding the gene – you don't cure it.

JILLIAN. I believe… This is what *I* believe. If we continue with the research we're doing, if people are willing to contribute to these studies, if everyone contributes, I believe that your children will have something akin to a cure. Or never get diabetes at all. You have children?

ARELLA. Yes, I have a daughter.

JILLIAN. Me too. Maybe if we find out what's causing this… Maybe your daughter, your daughter's daughter…

> *(long pause)*

ARELLA. I'll talk to the council.

> *(light shift)*

FOUR. The genetic anthropologist returned home from little Katie's party with Natalie and lots of party loot.

GRAHAM. How was it?

JILLIAN. Fantastic!!

GRAHAM. You're kidding. Are you sure you were in the right place?

JILLIAN. Four of the moms are going to get their genomes traced. Four out of fifteen! These women – you've been keeping them from me – man, they have money. Two of them are going for the whole thing. The whole sequence.

GRAHAM. Huh.

> (*to* NATALIE)

How was the party for you honey?

NATALIE. We all got My Little Ponies!

GRAHAM. That's amazing!

NATALIE. I got purple! And candy! And a bracelet! And a crown! And mommy was there! And two lollypops! And candy!

GRAHAM. Awesome!

JILLIAN. You were totally wrong about the books. The moms all said they would have loved signed copies.

GRAHAM. *(sighing)* OK, hon.

NATALIE. Her name is Stevie.

GRAHAM. It's a boy horse?

NATALIE. No, silly daddy!

She has to meet my other ponies!

> *(She runs off.)*

GRAHAM. Good idea!

JILLIAN. I'll do tomorrow's party too.

GRAHAM. Honey, I think it's a little weird for you to be pushing your…work at these events. It's really supposed to be about the kids, /you know?

JILLIAN. I wasn't pushing. Even the birthday kid's mom – Carol?

GRAHAM. Kristin.

JILLIAN. Even Kristin's interested. They were fascinated by it.

GRAHAM. It just doesn't seem like the right /time and place.

JILLIAN. A few of them were a little freaked out about the whole toxic knowledge thing.

(**FOUR** *and* **FIVE** *become mothers at the party.*)

FIVE. What if you find out you've got something awful and there's no cure for it? I'd rather not know. It would make me crazy.

JILLIAN. Doesn't it make you crazy *not* knowing? There might be something lurking in your genetic makeup, just waiting for its time. You're powerless if you don't know.

FIVE. But you're powerless anyway.

JILLIAN. Knowledge is power.

FIVE. I don't know.

(*to her daughter offstage*)

Brittney, honey – share. Everyone got two lollipops. Those are Chelsea's.

FOUR. So you did it? Got your genes done?

JILLIAN. In my lab. It's expensive, but I could do it for you too.

GRAHAM. You're like a pusher.

FOUR. (*to her daughter offstage*) Pick one that matches your crown, Jessica! Pink and orange don't go!

FIVE. Did you find anything? Is that too personal…

FOUR. That's better! Very pretty!

JILLIAN. I've got a mutation in the amyloid precursor protein, same as /my mother.

GRAHAM. What the hell, Jill??

JILLIAN. So I'm genetically destined to get early-onset/ Alzheimers.

GRAHAM. Why are you telling them this? These are Natalie's friend's mothers. They don't need to know this.

THREE. "She says whatever's on her mind. I love that."

FOUR. Oh my God. I'm so sorry. Does that mean you'll definitely...or is it just like statistically you're/more likely...

JILLIAN. It means I'll get it. By the time I'm 60. But maybe much sooner. It could have started at thirty.

GRAHAM. God, Jillian.

FIVE. God.

JILLIAN. It could be happening now.

FIVE. How are you even functioning? You're so brave. I'd just curl up in a corner and cry. Honestly. I would just give up.

> *(to her child)*

Brittney Ann, if I have to come over there you won't get *any* candies!

FOUR. I didn't even want the doctor to tell me if Jessica was a boy or a girl in advance! No, thank you, I said. I'll just be surprised.

FIVE. *(to her daughter)* Do you want to have to leave before the cake?

JILLIAN. My husband is like that. He won't let me find out if Natalie has the mutation.

GRAHAM. It's completely inappropriate for you to tell them about this!

THREE. "She says whatever's on her mind."

GRAHAM. Yeah yeah yeah.

THREE. "I love that."

FIVE. *Natalie* might have it?? You can tell at her age?

GRAHAM. You're going to affect how she's seen in the world. How her friends and their families treat her. It's terrible. You /can't be...

JILLIAN. Well, yes. If she has the same gene...

GRAHAM. She deserves to be who she wants to be. To tell her own story.

JILLIAN. ...it was there at birth.

GRAHAM. No more birthday parties for you. That's it. You're grounded.

FOUR. I have a good friend who did the testing because her father had Huntington's and it turned out she has it. Has the gene. They were just destroyed. Now the little time she has left is miserable. Why would you want to know?

JILLIAN. So I can do something about it! If I don't know I can't do anything!

FIVE. *Can* you do anything?

(to her daughter)

That's *it!* I'm counting to five. One. Two. Three. Good. OK. Good girl.

JILLIAN. There are drugs that might slow the disease. They're experimental, but I've been taking massive doses for years. Beta amyloids, statins, vitamin E, whatever – as soon as something comes out, any trial I can sign up for, I'm there. Probably it's not working, but I have to try at least.

FIVE. But aren't you worried about insurance companies finding out? Or your employers?

GRAHAM. Yes.

JILLIAN. Well, there are laws that they can't discriminate…

FIVE. I wouldn't trust them.

FOUR. Yeah, me either.

GRAHAM. Me either.

FOUR. No no no! Not in your nose!!

JILLIAN. It sounds crazy, but, in some ways, it's a gift. Now I know I'm in a race against time to get the work done, to get it done while I'm still functioning at, at optimal mental capacity. Every breakthrough I need to make I need to make *now*! *Now* is my time!

FIVE. Carpe diem!

JILLIAN. Right! And I'm betting on science. We're going to find a cure. I know it. Maybe before I get it. Certainly before Natalie gets it. If I can just get myself on the map –

NATALIE. *(from offstage)* Mommy!

JILLIAN. make some big strides so that I can get my own lab...

NATALIE. Mommy!

JILLIAN. I can really /put all my focus...

NATALIE. *Mommy!!!*

> (JILLIAN *finally realizes that she is the mommy being called. It's the first time in her life that someone has called to mommy, and it has been her. The enormity of that hits her.)*

JILLIAN. Oh! Natalie!

> *(She waves.)*

NATALIE. Hi, Mommy!!

JILLIAN. *(so touched)* Hi Natalie!

FIVE. Such a sweet girl, Natalie. Look how pretty with that purple against her dark skin.
She looks just like you.

JILLIAN. Like *me?*

FOUR. Yes, I see it too.

JILLIAN. Really? Everyone always says she looks exactly like Graham.

FOUR. No. I see you all over her.

FIVE. Your spitting image.

JILLIAN. Oh. That's so...

> *(very emotional)*

Thank you.

FIVE. Look – I'll give you my...blood, or my genes or whatever. Don't tell me what it says – I don't want to know. But...you can have it.

JILLIAN. That's wonderful!

> *(She hugs her impulsively.)*

FOUR. I'm gonna have to think about it…

JILLIAN. That's OK.

FIVE. But don't test Natalie… I really don't think you should.

JILLIAN. There's no way to protect her without knowing. I have to know.

GRAHAM. Well, you don't have to know.

(*dismissing* **FOUR** *and* **FIVE**)

Thanks. Thank you.

Because I'm her father and I refuse to have you look at her under a microscope.

JILLIAN. Well, it would be a printout, actually.

GRAHAM. We already decided this Jill. Why are you doing this? We agreed. It isn't fair.

JILLIAN. I didn't agree. I just stopped arguing.

(*Beat.* **GRAHAM** *is aghast.*)

Graham. What if there's some drug we could try? What if there were a trial we could do? Things are moving so fast, we have to be first in line.

GRAHAM. We're not trying an experimental drug on our four-year-old. Who might be perfectly fine.

JILLIAN. Or who might not be.

Look. I'm her mother and I deserve to know just as much as you deserve not to. I won't tell you if you prefer. I didn't tell you when I found out she was a girl.

GRAHAM. This is a lot different and you know it. I… absolutely…forbid it.

JILLIAN. You *forbid* it?

GRAHAM. Yes.

JILLIAN. Honey, we're not living in a Victorian novel. You can't /forbid things.

GRAHAM. I'm serious Jillian. I can't live with something like that. I can't handle it.

JILLIAN. I can't handle not knowing. Why should your fear be the thing that decides this?

NATALIE. *(entering)* Daddy's afraid? What are you afraid of Daddy?

GRAHAM. Nothing honey.

JILLIAN. Daddy is afraid that there are things to learn that might be scary.

GRAHAM. *Jillian!!*

JILLIAN. So he chooses not to know.

GRAHAM. What are you doing?

JILLIAN. But if you close your eyes when something's scary, it doesn't make it go away, does it? If you saw a bear, and you closed your eyes, the bear would eat you, right?

NATALIE. *What?*

GRAHAM. OK, that's enough.

JILLIAN. But if you learned everything you could about bears, and you knew what to do if you met one, you would stand a much better fighting chance.

GRAHAM. Natalie, honey. Mommy is just being silly.

NATALIE. What would I learn about bears?

GRAHAM. Mommy is just telling scary stories to be silly.

NATALIE. It would eat me?

(JILLIAN *grabs her and hugs her tight.*)

JILLIAN. I won't let it. I won't let it eat you.

NATALIE. Mommy! Too tight!

GRAHAM. Who wants to watch a movie?!

NATALIE. Really?!

GRAHAM. Sure! I'll put on a movie in our bedroom for you, while I talk to Mommy.

NATALIE. In the middle of the day?

JILLIAN. Just talk to me. I'm right here.

GRAHAM. It's a special treat! Come on. Let's put on a movie for you and Stevie!

NATALIE. Yayy!!

(*She hops on his back, horsie-style.*)

GRAHAM. *(to* JILLIAN, *pointedly)* I'll be right back.

*(They leave. JILLIAN gives the audience a look...
'now I'm in for it.')*

JILLIAN. All of this – these changes – genomics, it seems
so...unnatural. So scary. But it's really just the next
phase of our evolution.

*(We hear a children's movie starting up in the
other room.)*

Someday we'll be able to re-grow our hearts when our
hearts are failing, back up our memories every night
like we back up our computers. Someday we won't have
to live in terror that it's all running out.

GRAHAM. *(returning)* Listen, I don't want you talking about
all this in front of her. Our job is to protect her.

JILLIAN. And love her. And teach her.

GRAHAM. She's four. Maybe we can teach her about
crippling degenerative diseases when she's five.

JILLIAN. She's going to have to know.

GRAHAM. No she's not. That's ridiculous.

JILLIAN. She's going to have to know about me. Sooner or
later.

GRAHAM. Maybe it won't happen. Or maybe she'll be in
her forties when it starts. Maybe they'll find a cure.

JILLIAN. I think it's started, Graham.

GRAHAM. No.

JILLIAN. I'm losing words. I'm confused. My balance...

GRAHAM. You're over-tired. You're working too much.

JILLIAN. It seems different.

GRAHAM. It's because you're hyper-aware of it. That's the
problem with knowing. If you didn't know you would
just chalk it up to all the normal life pressures, which
is what it is.

JILLIAN. Maybe. Look, I want to have a chance to tell her
before I can't anymore. Nobody told me. Nobody
explained what was going on. I wasn't much older than
Natalie – my father was always at work. Little by little

she just wasn't my mother. She'd forget to pick me up from school. She'd forget to make meals. She'd leave the house without telling me where she was going for hours and hours. Started calling me other names.

FIVE. This is for you Jenny.

JILLIAN. Acting afraid suddenly, or angry. I didn't understand what was happening. If someone had only told me what was happening.

GRAHAM. I'm sorry, honey. I'm so sorry.

> *(He holds her for a moment.)*

That's not going to happen to Natalie. I promise you.

JILLIAN. OK.

GRAHAM. But let's let her be a little kid, OK? For now? If things change we'll talk about it. But for now...

JILLIAN. OK.

GRAHAM. Thanks.

> *(He holds her for a moment.)*

Make memories with her. That's what you can do for her.

JILLIAN. I'm not good at it. I don't know what to do.

GRAHAM. How about you do her bedtime story. That's my favorite time.

JILLIAN. I can't make up stories like you do.

GRAHAM. Then tell her real stories. Not scary real stories. But...real stories.

JILLIAN. ...OK.

GRAHAM. Good.

> *(They kiss.)*

JILLIAN. And I won't even tell you if I have her tested. I'll never tell you. You won't have to know.

> **(GRAHAM** *is too disheartened to say anything. Deep deep sigh.)*

> *(light shift)*

ARELLA. Arella Namida talked to the council. And convinced them to do the study.

> *(At the clinic in the Grand Canyon.* **JILLIAN** *is thrilled – it's finally happening! She makes a writing gesture to a tribe member.)*

JILLIAN. Sign right there. Thanks!

> *(to the audience)*

Every breakthrough in medicine has required a "yes."

> *(To someone who has given blood – she makes a handprint gesture.)*

OK. We just need your handprint. Right over there, at that table.

Study my blood, my tumor, my brain. We wouldn't have any of the medications we have now if people before us hadn't taken risks. Not an aspirin. Not a Tums.

> **(ARELLA** *tries to walk past unseen, but* **JILLIAN** *spots her.)*

Arella!

ARELLA. Yes. Hi.

JILLIAN. This is a wonderful turnout!

> *(To a tribe member. Signs writing.)*

Sign right here, thanks!

We'll probably come back every other week for a while. In case there's anyone who changes his mind, or is away.

ARELLA. No one is away.

JILLIAN. I guess – why would anyone ever leave here – it's so beautiful.

> *(to someone else)*

Right over there.

ARELLA. People do leave. I left for a time.

JILLIAN. You did?

ARELLA. I worked for the U.N. United Nations. On environmental issues. Right after college. I've traveled a good deal.

JILLIAN. I had no idea. I thought...

ARELLA. Yes. I know what you think.

JILLIAN. *(making a writing gesture to someone else)* You signed the consent form? Great!

> (**ARELLA** *watches her glee. To sober her:*)

ARELLA. Actually my sister is away now.

JILLIAN. Oh? Does she work /for the...

ARELLA. She's in the hospital. She's losing her leg.

JILLIAN. I'm sorry.

ARELLA. It's happening younger and younger. My grandmother reached sixty.
My mother died at forty-six.

JILLIAN. I'm really sorry, Arella.

ARELLA. I look at my daughter...

JILLIAN. I know.

ARELLA. *That's* why we're here.

JILLIAN. Right.

> (*There is a pause.*)

ARELLA. Take my blood.

JILLIAN. Oh! I didn't realize you hadn't given yet. Did you sign the consent form?

ARELLA. No.

JILLIAN. Here!

> (**ARELLA** *reads it. She looks at* **JILLIAN**. *Studies her for a moment.*)

Right there, at the bottom. And then Gary's almost free – he can help you. Gary!

ARELLA. No. I want you to take it.

JILLIAN. Oh. I don't do it. Myself. But the phlebotomists, they do it day and night so they're excellent.

ARELLA. Can you do it?

JILLIAN. Well, I can. I mean, I have, but...it's been years. Really, these guys are pros. It'll be faster and less painful. Believe me.

ARELLA. I want you to do it.

> *(She signs the form. Sits down. Bears her arm.)*

Take my blood.

JILLIAN. Yeah?

> *(beat)*

OK. Let me just...

> *(She gets the paraphernalia, nervously.)*

Let me see your arm. Ah! You have great veins. Luckily.

> *(She ties the tourniquet around ARELLA's arm.)*

Is that OK? Not too tight? OK. So...make a fist. Pump your hand like this. Wow, I haven't done this in a while. You're sure...

> *(ARELLA is sure.)*

This will pinch a little.

> *(She inserts the needle.)*

Whew! I got it! You can relax your hand. You've got great veins. Is that OK?

> *(ARELLA nods. JILLIAN attaches the tube, starts filling vials.)*

My mother died young too.

ARELLA. Diabetes?

JILLIAN. Alzheimer's. I was just a little kid.

ARELLA. Me too. My sister raised me. Well, the tribe raised me really.

JILLIAN. I don't have a tribe.

ARELLA. That's a hard thing. A little girl without a mother. There's strength in the tribe.

> *(beat)*

JILLIAN. Well, I believe we're all part of the same tribe, really. We're all related. I mean, distantly, but...you and I, we're really cousins.

(ARELLA *resists arguing.*)

ARELLA. You have family? You said you have a daughter?

JILLIAN. Yes. We actually have a lot in common, you and I.

(*Again,* ARELLA *just studies her.*)

Were you afraid to have offspring?

ARELLA. Afraid? No.

JILLIAN. Really? I was terrified.

ARELLA. Hm.

JILLIAN. And now – I know. I did the test and I have the mutation. I know I'm definitely going to get it. Early onset Alzheimers.

ARELLA. I'm sorry. That's a terrible thing to know.

(JILLIAN *finishes filling the vials, removes the needle. During the following she dabs with alcohol and puts on a bandage.*)

JILLIAN. There! You're all set! Hope that was okay.

ARELLA. I've never given my blood before. So I don't have a large means of comparison.

(*as* ARELLA *begins to walk away:*)

JILLIAN. Did you think about it? I mean, the risks? Before you decided to get pregnant?

ARELLA. Of course I thought about it. I think about it all the time. But I knew I wanted a child.

JILLIAN. Yeah, I think about it all the time too.

ARELLA. Yeah.

JILLIAN. And it's that double anxiety, right? The unimaginable – that she might get it. But also the thought of her seeing me go through it. You know? Like I did with my mom. I just don't want her to have to see that, watch me get more and more...

(*A wave of emotion.* **ARELLA** *puts a hand on* **JILLIAN***'s arm – a kindness that soaks into* **JILLIAN***'s whole body.*)

JILLIAN. Are you afraid to get close to her?

ARELLA. To Mona? What do you mean?

JILLIAN. For her to love you or need you too much? Because then, when you're sick, or...gone...

ARELLA. You're her mother. She needs you. Now.

(**JILLIAN** *hugs her. Awkwardly.* **ARELLA** *looks around to see if any of the tribe has noticed. They stand a moment.*)

JILLIAN. You know, if you ever wanted to come to the university...visit the lab... I would love to show you around. And then after...how old is Mona?

ARELLA. Seven.

JILLIAN. Ah. Natalie is four.

Well, if you come, visit the university I mean, you could come over for dinner after. I mean, your whole family could come, if you wanted. My husband's a really good cook.

(**ARELLA** *just studies her.*)

Anyway, here's my card, if you decide you ever want to...come.

(**ARELLA** *takes it.*)

ARELLA. It must be hard, not to have a tribe.

(*They stand together for a moment.*)

(*light shift*)

FOUR. The husband of the genetic anthropologist waited for Natalie at nursery school.

FIVE. Graham!

GRAHAM. Sheila! Hey! Joan!

FIVE. We finally got to meet Jillian! So lovely. It was wonderful to spend some time with her at little Katie's party.

GRAHAM. Yeah. She had fun too.

FIVE. She told us about your situation. I'm so sorry.

GRAHAM. Yes. She can be a little...boundaries are not her strong suit.

FIVE. Oh, I didn't realize it was something you /prefer not to...

GRAHAM. No, it's OK. /It's...

FOUR. Poor little Natalie.

GRAHAM. Well, no – it could be that she's fine. There's a good chance, an /excellent chance...

FOUR. You're both so brave. I'm praying for you.

FIVE. We all have our challenges. Our crosses to bear.

GRAHAM. Yup.

> *(light shift)*

THREE. The genetic anthropologist gave the social anthropologist some bad news.

KEN. You've checked and rechecked?

JILLIAN. There's no obvious linkage, Ken. I'm sorry.

KEN. Have you told the tribe?

JILLIAN. No. Not yet.

KEN. Maybe I should tell them.

JILLIAN. OK, but I'm still hopeful. I mean, obviously it would have been exciting to discover a direct link, but there are still so many more tests we should do. We found inbreeding coefficients for all members of the /tribe and...

KEN. You did studies on inbreeding?

JILLIAN. Sure.

KEN. There was no authority to do anything but diabetes studies.

JILLIAN. Ken, you know as well as I do that studying interbreeding and migratory patterns helps determine how isolated the /population is.

KEN. You studied migratory patterns? The tribe didn't authorize that. Would never have authorized that. Just saying there are migratory patterns is suggesting they didn't originate in the Canyon. It's attacking their creation story, their religious beliefs. Didn't you read my book?

JILLIAN. *(consent form)* Here. Here it is. They all signed this. To "study the causes of behavioral/medical disorders." Right here.

KEN. That's wildly vague.

JILLIAN. No. It's intentionally simple. English isn't their first language. You told me to make sure it would be /written in a way…

KEN. It's simple to the point of being meaningless.

JILLIAN. They were told to ask any questions – Arella was there to interpret. All the students were instructed to explain the project. We got both written and verbal consent. It's… Look, it's disappointing, but there are still a great number of important, positive results to be obtained from this study. There's already a lot of interest, several publications…

KEN. I don't want you publishing any of these findings. Or lecturing on them.

JILLIAN. Are you kidding? I did good science here. Finding the exact linkage…that was a /crapshoot.

KEN. I'm telling you. Don't publish this.

JILLIAN. *Nature* is publishing my paper in two months. Going through final revisions. And *Cell* is reviewing another.

KEN. Don't publish or I'll have to do something about it.

JILLIAN. You're threatening me?

KEN. I'm informing you.

JILLIAN. Well, I'm scheduled to give a talk next Thursday. At Cedar Hall.

KEN. Cancel it.

FIVE. Next Thursday. At Cedar Hall.

(JILLIAN *addresses the audience. She refers to slides on the screen.*)

JILLIAN. So, as you can see here...

TWO. Click.

JILLIAN. ...having obtained pedigrees tracing back to the late 1800s, there is a one to two percent interbreeding coefficient.

TWO. Click.

JILLIAN. As to geographical origins, eighteen blood samples from the tribe show that they originated in Eastern Asia. We estimate that their migration, crossing the Bering Strait to arrive in /North America around...

(ARELLA *is in the audience.*)

ARELLA. Did you get proper consent from the tribe to do this research?

JILLIAN. I'll be taking questions after the talk. I'll make sure to leave plenty /of time...

ARELLA. The tribe would not have consented to those studies.

JILLIAN. Excuse me?

Oh. Arella! I didn't know you'd be here.

And... Ken. Ah.

(*a moment to collect herself*)

As you know, you both know, I have a stack of consent forms.

ARELLA. You're saying we didn't come from the Canyon, that it's not our land. That we migrated here, like the Pilgrims.

JILLIAN. No. That's not why we trace geographical origins. I'm sorry. I'll be happy to talk to you afterward. Please stay after, OK?

(*She puts up the next slide.*)

TWO. Click.

JILLIAN. OK. As you can see here...

ARELLA. We didn't give you permission to make speeches, to say in public like this that we didn't come from the Grand Canyon. That we came from Asia. We would never have given our blood for that. For you to deny our beliefs.

JILLIAN. Arella, I told you we'd be studying the tribe's migratory patterns. It's an essential part of the work I do. We talked about it.

ARELLA. No. If the tribal council knew you would take our blood for this...

JILLIAN. You signed the consent form. You helped interpret for those who didn't understand. I thought it was clear.

DEAN HAGAN. *(walking on stage)* All right. We're going to adjourn this panel. Thank you all for coming.

       (**JILLIAN** *stands on stage stunned and confused.*)

       (light shift)

FOUR. Once upon a time

FIVE. In every city and every village

FOUR. In every country on every continent.

FIVE. In hundreds of languages.

FOUR. Right now! Right this very moment!

FIVE. Parents are telling their children the story

FOUR. Their children and their grandchildren

FIVE. They are telling the story

FOUR. The story of what it means to be alive.

       (**GRAHAM, JILLIAN** *and* **ARELLA** *are each telling their stories to their daughters, whom we don't see. They all have great love for their stories and their listeners.*)

GRAHAM. Once upon a time

ARELLA. When the earth was new

JILLIAN. In the beginning

GRAHAM. There was a princess, who lived in a magical kingdom. The princess was only four, but she was the smartest, funniest, kindest, *best singing*, most generous princess ever.

ARELLA. There were two gods of the universe, Hokomata and Tochopa. Tochopa had a little girl named Pukeheh that he loved so so so so much. Yes. Like I love you.

JILLIAN. You were just one tiny little Natalie cell. You were such a teeny tiny little Natalie cell, you could only be seen with a microscope!

GRAHAM. One day

ARELLA. One morning

GRAHAM. ...a fierce, frightening, fire-breathing dragon came to the princess's land. None of the knights could drive the dragon away! None of the swordsmen could slay it! But, the little princess said, let me sing to the dragon!

ARELLA. The two gods had a terrible fight, and Hokomata said, "I will make a flood to drown the earth!" So, to survive the flood, Tochopa hid his daughter in a hollow log.

JILLIAN. That tiny little Natalie cell divided so there were two cells! And then four Natalie cells! And dividing and dividing until... Guess how many cells you are now?
Hah! Even more than six! Even more than seven! Want me to tell you?

ARELLA. The flood made two great rushing rivers that made... Right! Chi-a-mi-mi! The Grand Canyon!

JILLIAN. You are...ten trillion cells!

ARELLA. After the flood, Pukeheh emerged from her hiding place in the log. She lived to see the new world. But she was all alone. So, the sun gave Pukehehe a son, In-ya-a, which means...the son of the Sun!

GRAHAM. The king and queen said – No! We will run away and live in the woods rather than let you meet that fearful dragon! But the little princess said, no, mother and father, we must face our dragons. And she started to sing a sweet melody.

JILLIAN. What are these letters? Can you tell me? Right! A T C G! Copying and copying and copying.

ARELLA. Pukeheh loved her son, but she wanted to have a little girl too. A mighty waterfall gave her that little girl! That's why all our girls are called... Daughters of the Water.

JILLIAN. Now, when I copy things again and again and again, I goof up. I forget to cross a T. Or I put a C where a G should be.

GRAHAM. As she sang, the dragon, who had been growling and roaring and hissing great flames, grew quiet. The whole kingdom held its breath, when outside came the sound of snorting and screeching. It was the dragon. And he was singing!

JILLIAN. And this A T C G is being copied billions of times! Can you imagine how many goofs might happen?

ARELLA. These two children brought forth the whole of the human race.

JILLIAN. So what's amazing isn't the typos and glitches and goofs. What's amazing is how often it turns out right!

ARELLA. We were assigned guardians of the Grand Canyon.

JILLIAN. With all those chances for things to go terribly wrong, here we are! We made it! We're alive!

GRAHAM. And all the kingdom let out a cheer as the little princess petted the dragon's snout.

ARELLA. And so, our people lived in the Grand Canyon for all time, in peace.

GRAHAM. And they all lived together in peace, happily ever after.

JILLIAN. And we're together. So lucky to be here, together.

(*We hear* **NATALIE***'s voice.*)

NATALIE. Mommy, is that a true story?

JILLIAN. It's one hundred percent verifiably true!

NATALIE. I love you Mommy.

JILLIAN. *(A beat. Overwhelmed:)* Oh my goodness. You have no idea – you have no idea how much I love you, Natalie.

(light shift)

TWO. The dean of the large university in Arizona called the two anthropologists into her office.

DEAN HAGAN. They want their blood back. They're willing to come to the university to get it.

JILLIAN. It isn't all here.

KEN. Where is it?

JILLIAN. It's in labs and universities all over the country. We don't do all the testing/ here.

KEN. Goddammit Jillian!

JILLIAN. I thought you knew that.

DEAN HAGAN. I'm stunned, Dr. Elliott, at how careless you've been. How /negligent.

JILLIAN. I wasn't careless. This is how science is done. This is how...this is how every lab in the... /in the...

DEAN HAGAN. Get the blood back. Now.

JILLIAN. I'm not sure I can.

DEAN HAGAN. You don't seem to understand how serious this is. They're going to sue. They have the financial support of several wealthier tribes. Tribes with casino money. If we can get them their blood back, if we can promise not to publish any more articles, no more lectures...

JILLIAN. I have an article coming out in *Nature*! There's been important work /done here.

KEN. We've contacted *Nature* and *Cell* – the publications are on hold.

JILLIAN. What??

DEAN HAGAN. If they go forward with this lawsuit it could cost us millions.

JILLIAN. I can't believe this, Ken. You...sabotaged me. I was trying to help the tribe. We didn't find that one link to diabetes, but we did testing /that might find other contributing factors.

KEN. They didn't give you permission to do those other tests! Don't you understand this? You violated their trust.

JILLIAN. It did them no harm. /There was no...

KEN. You've humiliated them! You publically contradicted their creation story.

DEAN HAGAN. You weren't authorized to trace their geographical origins to begin with.

JILLIAN. That's what I do!

KEN. You were the wrong person to come to with this. I acknowledge my fault in that. Trusting you with this.

JILLIAN. If they believe that they came from the Grand Canyon, what does it matter what I say? Their beliefs, which they've had for centuries, must be sturdier than that.

KEN. This is the attitude. /This is...

JILLIAN. What if I'd proven that they did come from the canyon– if I'd confirmed their story, then my research would have been welcome?

KEN. You put my relationship with the tribe in jeopardy, a relationship I've nurtured for forty years. They're like family to me.

DEAN HAGAN. Look. You fix this. Period. This could have the NIH breathing down our necks. They could hold up grants for hundreds of millions of dollars, you understand? Money that pays the overhead at the hospital. Money that goes towards studies with other vulnerable populations. Scientific research projects that are of much higher priority than this. Do you understand? Not to mention our international reputation.

We have students coming from all over the world for our Native studies. Our /reputation...

JILLIAN. I'll talk to the tribe I'll tell them what I've been doing. /Why.

KEN. Don't go near the tribe. Except to return their blood.

JILLIAN. But if I could explain to Arella, she'd understand. If I /had a chance to...

KEN. You had your chance to explain. You had a chance to get their consent. If you'd asked for it, who knows, maybe they would have allowed you to do all kinds of testing. But you didn't ask.

JILLIAN. Truly informed consent for genomic research, *truly* informed, would require putting each one of them through med school. Things are changing so fast. *I* can barely keep up. What we can do – what we can discover in a blood sample this month may be a scrap of what we can learn a month from now. We just don't know what we'll know. There's no way to fully represent what we might look for.

DEAN HAGAN. Then you don't look. You don't do the testing.

JILLIAN. What if I found a gene for something curable – some easily treatable cancer? Should I ignore it because that wasn't on the consent form?

DEAN HAGAN. Yes. If they didn't agree that you should look for it. Yes.

JILLIAN. If I see they have some curable disease I should just ignore it?

DEAN HAGAN. If that's what you agreed to.

JILLIAN. That's terrible.

DEAN HAGAN. People have a right to decide what they want to know. Or not know.

KEN. And you didn't find anything of benefit to the tribe.

JILLIAN. Not yet! But I still might. Let me keep looking!

DEAN HAGAN. There's nothing more for you to look at. You're returning the blood. You're doing everything you can to make this right. And just pray that this thing doesn't go to court.

(light shift)

THREE. The genetic anthropologist went home early that day.

(JILLIAN *sits at home with her head in her hands.*)

GRAHAM. Oh God. Why are you home? She has it. You found out.

JILLIAN. No.

GRAHAM. No? Oh God.

JILLIAN. No. The tribe wants me to stop the research. They want their blood back.

GRAHAM. Why?

JILLIAN. They think it's sacred. That I betrayed them.

GRAHAM. What?

JILLIAN. And my *Cell* article. *Nature.* They've put my articles on hold.

GRAHAM. They think you betrayed them?

JILLIAN. People don't get how science works! They think we single-mindedly do experiments, knowing what we'll find, and then we get the answer. But real science is in the mistakes. It's searching, not knowing what we're even looking for, and then stumbling across the truth. That's how huge discoveries are made. That's how we change the world.

GRAHAM. How did you betray them?

JILLIAN. I thought they understood. That I'd be testing for a lot of things.

GRAHAM. What were you testing for?

JILLIAN. Everything! That's my work! Search for the truth. Find out who we really are. The whole story is there to be read, we don't understand even a fraction of it yet, and they want me to only read every fourth line. Maybe I could save this tribe, it's possible, but they're more interested in hanging on to ancient myths than looking at what's really there.

GRAHAM. But… I mean, they have their own ideas about who they are, right?

JILLIAN. What?

GRAHAM. Their own story. Right? This tribe…

JILLIAN. What??

GRAHAM. They're already in such a vulnerable position. Right? I think it might be hard for you to understand how people of color, who have been constantly /subjected to…

JILLIAN. Wait. You're making this about race now?

GRAHAM. Well, it's not *just* about race.

JILLIAN. It's not about race to me at all.

GRAHAM. Well, you have that luxury.

JILLIAN. Wow.

(*Long moment while they both absorb this.*)

GRAHAM. You know, I walked in, I saw you sitting there – I was sure you were home because you'd had Natalie tested. You'd found out.

JILLIAN. Nope.

GRAHAM. Then you haven't?

JILLIAN. Graham. You said you don't want to know.

GRAHAM. But I see you, you're home early, and my heart stops.

JILLIAN. I don't know what to do about that.

GRAHAM. Did you have her tested yet?

(*She gives him a long look.*)

What would it entail?

JILLIAN. Really?

GRAHAM. Just tell me that. What would you do? Would you have to take blood?

JILLIAN. If I wanted a complete screening, I would need blood. But, I only want to look for that one gene.

GRAHAM. So…how would you do it?

JILLIAN. I'd just need a swab. Inside her cheek.

GRAHAM. Oh my God.

JILLIAN. What?

GRAHAM. There would be no sign. Not even a bandaid. You could have already done it. And I'd have no idea.

JILLIAN. Graham. I told you the first day we met I was terrified to have a child. And why. I…*informed* you.

GRAHAM. What are you saying – you wish we hadn't had Natalie?

JILLIAN. What??

GRAHAM. No. I'm sorry.

JILLIAN. I can't live with the uncertainty. But I won't tell you. I won't tell you if she has it. I won't tell you if I've done the testing.

GRAHAM. Have you done it yet?

(She just looks at him.)

Oh my God, Jill.

(Piecing this together. How is he going to live with this every day?)

You know, it's always been…the highlight of our day… when you come home from work. When we hear your car pull up. Now, every time you walk through that door… I'll be dreading it. I'll be scanning your face for some sign. How will I ever be able to look at you again, without wondering what you know?

(They both sit with this.)

(light shift)

FOUR. Once again, ignoring the wishes of the social anthropologist, the genetic anthropologist went to see Arella Namida.

JILLIAN. Don't give up! There are still more tests we should do.

ARELLA. I had to go door to door and explain what you'd done. That I was wrong to ask for their trust. My uncle, he's the strongest man I've ever known. The bravest.

He cried when I told him what you'd done with our blood. That you betrayed us.

JILLIAN. Arella, I would never betray you. I'm your friend. Everything I was doing, everything I mean to do is to find out the truth, to find out genetically what might be harming your tribe. And then see if we can change the future. For your daughter. For my daughter. I'm trying to save them.

ARELLA. You stood up in an auditorium full of strangers and talked about my people. Told them your lies about us.

JILLIAN. But, they're not lies.

    (beat)

ARELLA. What if it were taken from you? Where you come from. Who you are. The deepest truth about your life. What if that were taken from you?

JILLIAN. It is. I'm losing my story

ARELLA. We lost our land. We lost our culture. We lost our independence. We lost our health. We lost everything. What we had left was who we are and where we come from.

We sprang forth from the Grand Canyon. That was what we had left.

JILLIAN. *(fully stricken with how she's hurt her)* I'm sorry, Arella.

    (She wrestles with herself about whether to persist. But…she must.)

But…

What you have left…

    (A breath. She must.)

What you have left is your daughter. What will you do to save her? What will you do? There's still hope. There's still a chance if you give me more time.

I would do ANYTHING to save Natalie. I would sacrifice whatever I had to sacrifice. My job. My marriage. My life. If I thought it would save her.

JILLIAN. *(cont.)* Give me more time, Arella.

ARELLA. We're taking back our blood. It's over. Stop giving your talks about us. And never come here again.

> *(light shift)*

FOUR. The genetic anthropologist gave a talk about the origins of informed consent.

JILLIAN. We first passed laws on informed consent after World War II, the...the...

> *(She pauses, shaken. Looks at her cards but nothing looks familiar.)*

> *(In whispers all around her, that she can't quite hear, the thoughts in her mind that can't quite connect:)*

TWO. The Nuremburg

THREE. Nuremburg

FOUR. Nuremburg

FIVE. Nuremberg Code.

JILLIAN. Yes. The... Nuremberg... We passed laws to ensure that terrible...harms to people – like the so-called "experiments" that the Nazis performed... To make sure that wouldn't happen. Again. Or...or also the...

> *(She looks through her cards again. Beat.)*

> *(Whispered, barely audible, overlapping:)*

THREE. The Tuskegee Study /of Untreated Syphilis in the African American Male.

FOUR. Tuskegee

FIVE. Tuskegee

TWO. Tuskegee

JILLIAN. Yes. Thank you. The Tuskegee...this was...to discover what would happen if syphilis went untreated, and...four hundred men...they were told that there would be "special free treatment." But in fact...what they did was... Sorry. What they did... They gave them... Sorry.

(She looks through her cards.)

(Whispered, overlapping:)

TWO. Spinal taps.

THREE. Spinal taps

FOUR. Spinal taps

FIVE. Spinal taps

JILLIAN. Spinal taps. Yes. They gave them spinal taps. So...those things were terrible. Terrible abuses of people, of their rights, and also, of course, it did them great harm. Actual...physical and... That is what informed consent is...why we have it...to prevent...

> *(There is a pause. **JILLIAN** looks to the other actors, but they don't know where she's going with this, and can't help her.)*

> *(She's lost. She goes back to what she knows. In desperation.)*

We're all related. We're all in this together. Cousins. Scientists...don't mean harm. Real scientists. We mean...to do good.

> *(light shift)*

FOUR. The dean of the large university in Arizona consulted many lawyers.

DEAN HAGAN. They're filing their suit. No one from the university is ever to set foot on their reservation again. They're suing for twenty-five million dollars.

JILLIAN. /Twenty-five million.

DEAN HAGAN. It's going to cost a million dollars to fight this thing. And that's if we win.

FOUR. *(a lawyer)* Your honor, there are six causes of action. One.

DEAN HAGAN. Dr. Elliot.

LAWYER. Lack of informed consent. Not having appropriate procedures for people whose main language was the tribal language.

DEAN HAGAN. There is no chance that the committee on academic /promotions...

JILLIAN. /No! Dean Hagan. Please.

LAWYER. Two. Fraud and misrepresentation.

DEAN HAGAN. Will approve of you getting /tenure.

JILLIAN. Please /don't fire me

LAWYER. Three. Intentional or negligent infliction of emotional /distress.

JILLIAN. /Don't fire me.

LAWYER. Four. Conversion.

DEAN HAGAN. I suggest that you /start making other plans.

LAWYER. Five. Violation of civil /rights.

DEAN HAGAN. *(morphing into Mother, trying to unhook her pendant)* Jenny, you should have this. This should go to you.

JILLIAN. I have so much /work to do. Please. Give me more time. I need more time.

LAWYER. And Six. Negligence, gross negligence, and negligence /per se.

DEAN HAGAN. The best thing to redeem the university's reputation would be for you to leave.

> *(Light shift. **GRAHAM** is there. She goes to him.)*

JILLIAN. It's over.

GRAHAM. Oh, honey.

JILLIAN. My job. My lab. My articles. All gone.
I can't save her, Graham. I'll never have my own lab. I'll never study Alzheimer's full time. I can't save her.

GRAHAM. You're amazing. You'll get another job. You'll get your own lab. It could still /happen.

JILLIAN. There's no time. I'm out of time.

GRAHAM. I'm so sorry, honey.

> *(He holds her.)*

It's all going to be OK.

> *(They sit with this for a long time.)*

JILLIAN. I haven't had her tested, Graham. I'm not going to have her tested.

GRAHAM. No?

JILLIAN. I don't want you to have to look at me and wonder what I know. I want you to look at me and see *me*.

(*He kisses her.*)

And, there's nothing I can do now. I'm so…helpless. There's nothing I can do for her.

GRAHAM. There's so much you can do.

JILLIAN. No.

(*pause*)

GRAHAM. We'll both take her to the party this weekend.

JILLIAN. *Another* party?

GRAHAM. Another princess party.

(*beat*)

JILLIAN. OK.

GRAHAM. And we'll take her to the zoo. And the planetarium. And the park. And we'll teach her how to tie her shoelaces, and how to divide, and how to bounce back when someone hurts her feelings.

JILLIAN. I'll just kill them.

GRAHAM. OK, honey.

(*They kiss.*)

There's so much we can do.

(*light shift*)

FOUR. And then the tribe took back what they could take back. They collected their blood.

(**JILLIAN** *watches as the tribe files in to collect their blood, which is in a large icebox marked "Elliott." They are singing a tribal song.* **TWO** *stands holding* **FIVE**, *who is softly crying.*)

(**ARELLA** *and* **THREE** *remove the vials of blood from the icebox and wrap them in a ceremonial* *cloth. There is great ritual to it. They all turn to look at* **JILLIAN** *together, and then leave.)*

FOUR. And then the genetic /anthropologist…

JILLIAN. Wait.

Wait.

(She goes to the empty box. Takes a moment to process this.)

Memory. Is a physical thing. It's little traces of protein in your brain making connections to another part of your brain. We build a memory. We construct it.

(to the audience)

Right now, right this second, each of us, we're building a memory. Writing the story of our lives, as we're living it. As we're telling and retelling it. Not one of us will remember the story of what happened today in the same way. Or…even in the way it actually happened.

(Coming down to them – really asking the audience…)

Who are you, really? Are you the person you see when you look in the mirror? Are you your job? What you create? What you destroy? *Are* you your genome? Or are you your memories.

And when your memory fades…who are you then?

OK. I'm ready.

(She returns to **NATALIE***'s letter, from the top of the play.)*

(On the screen is **JILLIAN***'s genome sequence. Softly, they read off the sequence in pairs.)*

TWO. TA

FOUR. GC

FIVE. CG

THREE. AT

FIVE. GC

JILLIAN. Dear Natalie,

> *(To the genome sequence:)*

Stop!

You're reading this letter because I've forgotten the things I want to tell you. Today, the day I'm writing this, today is the day that matters. Today I can look at you, and know you're my little girl, and you're perfect. Not a perfect little girl. Nobody is a perfect little girl. But you're perfect to me.

I hope you know how much I love you. I hope you have my pendant and that you wear it, always. I hope if one day I look at you and don't know you, you realize that I'm gone. When that happens, you can be sad that your Mommy died. And then don't come back again. I don't want you to see me like that. It's not me.

Natalie. There are stories of our family, of where we come from, that I mean to tell you. That you might tell your little girl some day.

And there are stories in our makeup, in our cells, ancient stories – but right now they're much better at ⁻ glimpsing the past than predicting the future.

TA GC CG AT GC

That's not who we are. That's not our future. We decide who we are. We have our own stories to tell. Tell your own story.

Once upon a time…

End of Play

CPSIA information can be obtained
at www.ICGtesting.com
Printed in the USA
LVHW081524261219
641750LV00012B/1391/P

9 780573 799860